CHRISTMAS ALREADY AGAIN YET

Notice anything?

Gray Jolliffe

CHRISTMAS ALREADY AGAIN YET

ARROW BOOKS

To Al, without whom
this book would have been thinner.

Arrow Books Limited
62–65 Chandos Place, London WC2N 4NW

An imprint of Century Hutchinson Ltd

London Melbourne Sydney Auckland
Johannesburg and agencies throughout the world

Christmas Already first published by Essex House Publishers 1978
Arrow edition first published 1982
Reprinted 1983 and 1984
This revised edition first published 1987

Illustrations and text © Gray Jolliffe 1978, 1982 and 1987

Typeset by JH Graphics Ltd, Reading, Berks
Colour separation by Dot Gradations,
South Woodham, Ferrers, Essex
Printed and bound in Great Britain by
Scotprint Ltd, Musselburgh, Scotland

ISBN 0 09 947830 7

Bit of a tricky one this. We want a Jewish gag-book about Christmas - mildly offensive but not over the top, light but uncompromising, no filth - a bit naughty, but don't overdo it. Get the picture.
BRIEF

Business is terrible. Somehow we have to make a
little prophet.

Knock up a man's wife? What kind of angel would agree
to do a thing like that?

How else do you expect a reindeer to fly?

You're asking me to be a surrogate mother for no money?
You have got to be kidding!

Of *course* he's gay! Do you think I'm a virgin because
I like it?

So this is where you get your red nose!

You want a Filofax? Do me a favour! What kind of
reindeer would use a Filofax.

Take it easy, Romeo! First you have to buy me dinner.

And you tell God you were lucky to get away with a black eye.

I reckon you could get down 50 per cent more chimneys if you got
down 50 per cent less booze.

It was great babe, but now I gotta fly.

Hold it, Superman – you dropped one of your flip flops.

Tell you what, sunshine – let's have a couple more and
miss out Poland.

You're just like all the others.

OK, pregnant is only a *few* lousy months,
but this I have to wear all my life?

We better get this show on the road. Who's driving, you or me?

And here's one for the kid when he arrives . . . size one.

Oh, and there's just one other thing, Sharon. God would
like you to change your name to Mary.

Sorry boss, my mistake. The bicycle was for next door.

Well don't just stand there looking at it.

New gown? Different lipstick? Okay, I give up . . .
what's different?

I'm pregnant, you old faggot. Figure that one out!

I don't care who you are — just don't you come one step
closer, you dirty little man.

Alright already, so I do go out more than once a year.

What do you *mean* I can't be. I am, and you better believe it.

Weirdest thing I ever saw – a pregnant virgin with a frisbee on her head.

It's Christmas, I'm pregnant, God knows how – and now
you tell me you forgot to book a room. Terrific!

My accountant is right — I should franchise this bit.

I'm sorry sir, but we simply do not have a room. Even
for a gold credit card.

My own son - married to a Shikse - celebrating Christmas!
A joint of ham in the fridge!
You buy everything retail! You never wear your Yarmulkeh!
Tell your Momma one thing bubeleh - are you still circumcised?
1
2
3
4

Smith? That's a new one. Most of them put 'Cohen'.

There's no room service, but you'll find a mini-bar under that pile of rubbish!

Oh gawd, it's at Bernie's place – that's a bad start!

So three months ago I say 'Are you positive the annexe
will be finished by Christmas?' But you know builders.

Try winding on, idiot.

The lease says 'no animals' so leave the talking to me.

Well at least the conception was immaculate!

Hurry up? Listen – next time *you* carry the gold!

Yes, I'm sure you've had no complaints, but that's not
what I meant when I asked if you'd been good.

All this going on and you can *eat*?

Jesus? Why would you want to give him a Puerto Rican name?

JC? How lovely! I'm AC and he's AC/DC.

This year we'll do it the easy way and give them what
they really want.

Where in God's name have you been?

A Capricorn yet! I too am a Capricorn!
God's children, us Capricorns!

So what do you expect with a one-star hotel?

Thinking about it, we'd save a lot of time if instead of
crawling back up the chimney you simply let yourself
out of the front door

No, idiot, I asked for a mounted photo of Rudolph, not
a photo of Rudolph mounted.

It's always tough on a kid having his birthday and Christmas
all on the same day.

Frankincense and myrrh we have more than we can shake a stick
at already. But the gold is very nice.

Santa Claus? No bubeleh, I'm Santa Cohen.
Wanna buy a present?

Ask yourself, Mr Claus – how can I justify a further facility
to someone who appears so consistently in the red?

It's supposed to be frankincense, but don't be too surprised
if you find a Tonka Toy in there.

And finally – a life subscription to his trade journal.

Relax, Sharon – it's me, Solly Strumpfenberg!

Okay, okay, Libya, but I'm telling you – you'll *hate* it!

He's here to save mankind? Well, mazeltov, though personally
I don't fancy his chances.

There's no point trying to deny paternity, Joseph – look
at that nose!

Nope, bicycles, guitars, drum kits, rowing machines, but
not a single full-size snooker table.

Of course the *real* joke is he's not even the father!

It's unbreakable plastic. Nice, huh?

Well of *course* it's home made! You ever tried buying branded
whisky in the Bible Belt?

This is the part that always makes *me* smile.

C'mon boss – it's gone four and we've still got Africa to do.

Do you know who that *is* out there? That's Mr and Mrs Christ
and their son the Saviour! And where do you put them? In
the goddam stable, you klutz! Five martinis on the house
is how you say sorry

'No room,' I say. 'So can we stay in the stable?' 'Okay,'
I say, 'but what about the animals and the smell?' 'You
obviously haven't met my husband,' she says.

I don't remember a Christmas where he didn't get like this,
the bum!

Well, we must be off now . . . see you next Christmas maybe?

'Not the father?' I said. 'Then who is? An angel? . . .
You're putting me on!'

Tell her I got it wholesale and you'll have more than a red nose.

An ordinary kid? So if he's just an ordinary kid, what's
this – a bagel?

They even sang one called 'Camel ye Faithful'.

Sorry love, but a framed print of Barry Manilow was the only
thing I had left.

Trade in? With 93903472143996571800927301 miles on the clock?
Do me a favour!

Already he's started!

This is positively the last Christmas I'm spending with your family.

Now they tell us.

That's right – Father Christmas. Don't tell me you don't
celebrate Christmas in these parts.

. . . And next Christmas you take me to Eilat, OK?

One day, bubeleh, I want you should do your Momma a
favour – work a miracle on your Poppa.

It's our first night in the new job — boy, what a shlep!

Why didn't you *say* you were having a Messiah? I would have given you the penthouse suite.

2.

3

4

Last stop Rio! Good thinking, Rudie!

If you'd been there, you could have had one.

That's no carpenter. *That* is an intellectual!

Hi, you guys! What are we having for Christmas din . . .

Gone out? Have you checked the batteries?